How Toys Work

Levers

Siân Smith

www.raintreepublishers.co.uk
Visit our website to find out
more information about
Raintree books.

To order:
☎ Phone 0845 6044371
📄 Fax +44 (0) 1865 312263
🖳 Email myorders@raintreepublishers.co.uk

Customers from outside the UK please telephone +44 1865 312262

Raintree is an imprint of Capstone Global Library Limited,
a company incorporated in England and Wales having its
registered office at 7 Pilgrim Street, London, EC4V 6LB
– Registered company number: 6695582

Edited by Dan Nunn, Rebecca Rissman, and Sian Smith
Designed by Joanna Hinton-Malivoire
Picture research by Mica Brancic
Production by Victoria Fitzgerald
Originated by Capstone Global Library Ltd
Printed and bound in China by South China Printing Company Ltd

ISBN 978 1 4062 3798 6
16 15 14 13 12
10 9 8 7 6 5 4 3 2 1

British Library Cataloguing in Publication Data
Smith, Sian.
Levers. -- (How toys work)
1. Levers--Juvenile literature.
I. Title II. Series
621.8-dc22

Acknowledgements
The author and publisher are grateful to the following for
permission to reproduce copyright material: Alamy pp. 14, 17
(© Finnbarr Webster); © Capstone Global Library Ltd pp.7, 20,
21 (Lord and Leverett), 5, 6, 8, 9, 10, 11, 13, 18, 19, 22c, 23
top (Karon Dubke); iStockphoto pp.16, 23 bottom (© Sergey
Lavrentev); Shutterstock pp.4 (© Peteri), 4 bottom left (© Elena
Schweitzer), 4 top left (© Jiri Hera), 4 top right (© Adi), 12
(© axle71), 15 (© Warren Goldswain), 22a (© Foong Kok Leong),
22b (© Barnaby Chambers); 22d (© Perseo Medusa).

Cover photograph of a boy and a girl on a see-saw reproduced
with permission of Shutterstock (© Warren Goldswain). Back cover
photograph of a game reproduced with permission of © Capstone
Publishers (Karon Dubke).

We would like to thank David Harrison, Nancy Harris, Dee Reid,
and Diana Bentley for their assistance in the preparation of
this book.

Every effort has been made to contact copyright holders of
material reproduced in this book. Any omissions will be rectified in
subsequent printings if notice is given to the publisher.

Contents

Different toys

There are many different kinds
of toys.

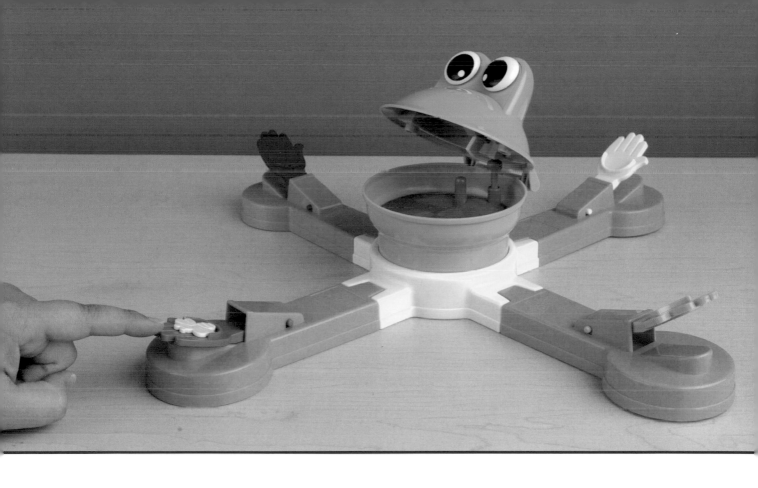

Toys work in different ways.

Levers

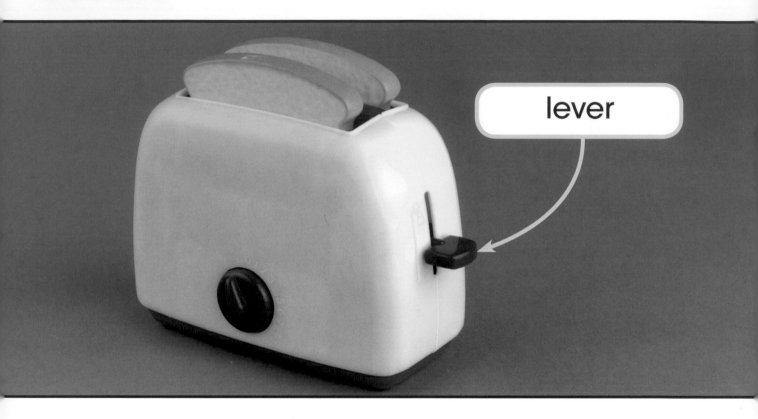

lever

Some toys use levers to work.

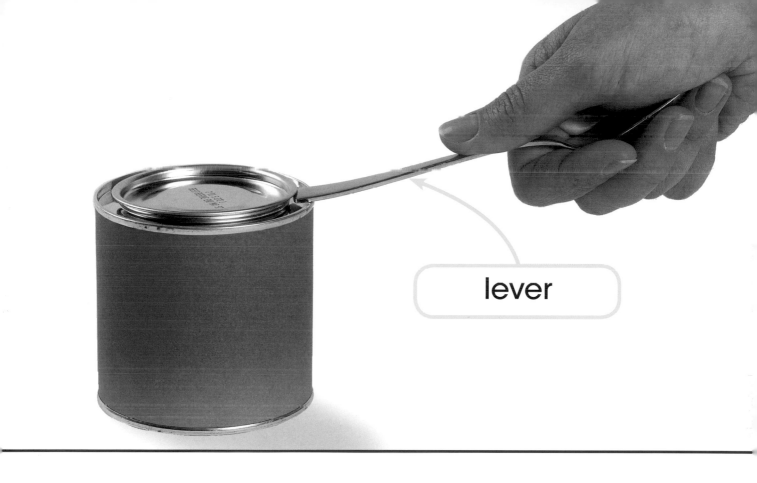

lever

A lever can be a hard stick or bar.

A lever can make things easy
to move.

push

We push or pull a lever.

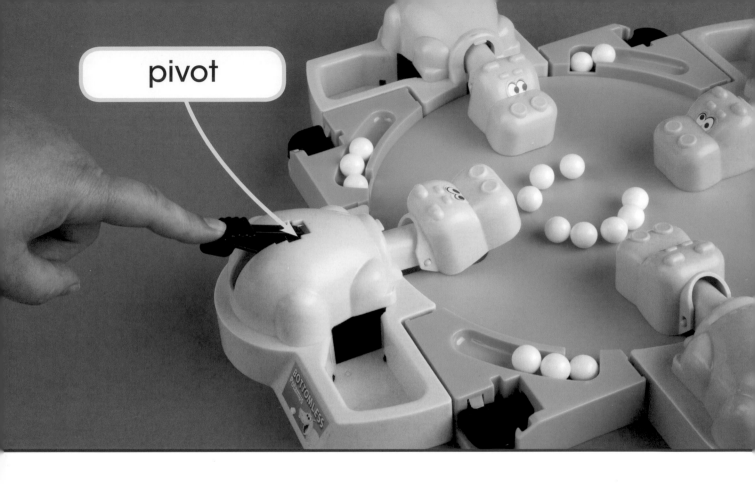

pivot

The lever turns at a place called
a pivot.

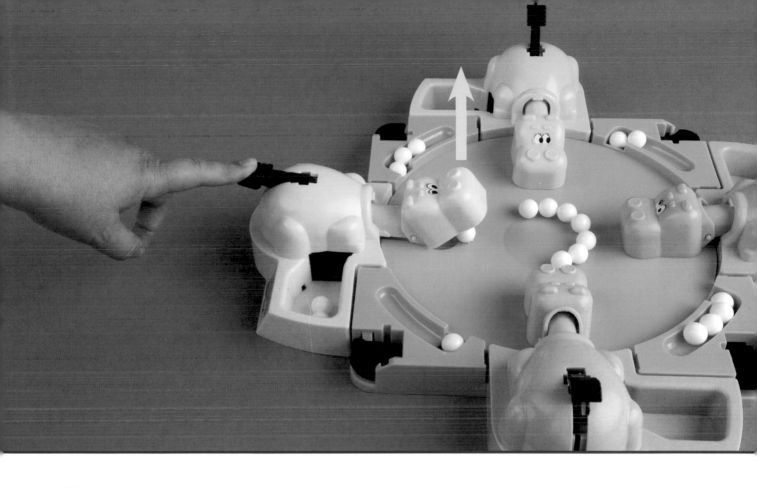

The lever makes something move.

More toys with levers

A toy spade is a type of lever.

Your hand turns the spade to lift
up sand.

A see-saw is a type of lever.

pivot

A see-saw turns in the middle.

When we sit on one end, we push
it down.

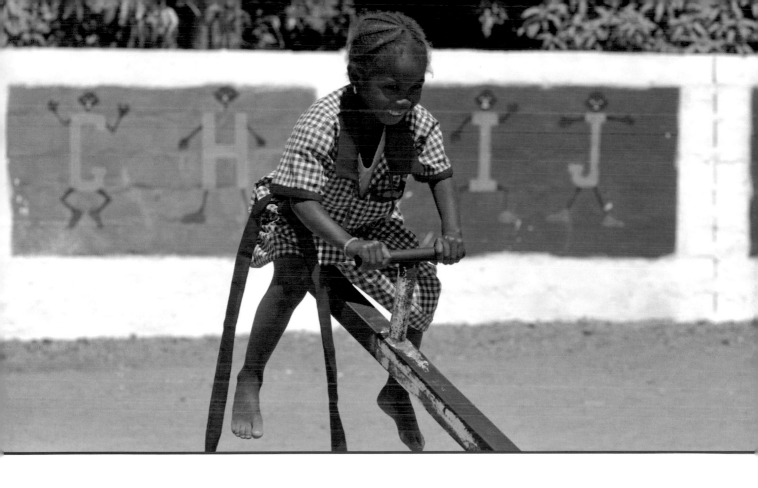

This pushes the other end up.

lever

This digger uses a lever.

shovel

You pull the lever to move the shovel.

lever

This toy uses a lever.

You push the lever to move
the arms.

Quiz

a

b

c

d

Which one of these toys uses a lever to work?

Answer on page 24

Picture glossary

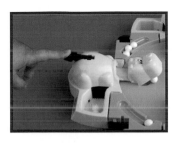

lever a lever is used to make something move. Many levers are shaped like bars or rods.

pivot the name given to the place where something turns

Index

Answer to question on page 22: Toy c uses a lever to work.

Notes for parents and teachers

Introduction
Show the children a collection of toys. One or more of the toys should have a lever mechanism. Ask the children if they can spot the toy with the lever. Do they know what a lever is and what it does?

More information about levers
Explain that a lever is a tool we use that helps us to make something move. Levers also make it easier for us to lift or move heavy things. Many levers are shaped like a stick or bar. You push or pull a lever at one end, and it makes something move in the middle or at the other end of the lever. Demonstrate a lever in action. Explain that the place where a lever turns is called a pivot (it is also called a fulcrum).

Follow up activities
Encourage the children to look around their homes to find one example of a lever. Ask them to draw this or bring it in so that these examples can be shared. For more advanced work on simple machines, children can work with an adult to discuss and play the games at: www.edheads.org/activities/simple-machines